Instant Pentaho Data Integration Kitchen

Explore the world of Pentaho Data Integration command-line tools which will help you use the Kitchen

Sergio Ramazzina

BIRMINGHAM - MUMBAI

Instant Pentaho Data Integration Kitchen

First published: July 2013

Production Reference: 1240713

Published by Packt Publishing Ltd.
Livery Place
35 Livery Street
Birmingham B3 2PB, UK.

ISBN 978-1-84969-690-6

www.packtpub.com

Credits

Author

Sergio Ramazzina

Reviewer

Joel Latino

Acquisition Editor

Erol Staveley

Commissioning Editor

Shreerang Deshpande

Technical Editor

Sampreshita Maheshwari

Copy Editor

Insiya Morbiwala

Project Coordinator

Suraj Bist

Proofreader

Paul Hindle

Production Coordinator

Zahid Shaikh

Cover Work

Prachali Bhiwandkar

Cover Image

Aditi Gajjar

About the Author

Sergio Ramazzina is a software architect/trainer with over 20 years of experience working on a large number of projects for banks and major Italian companies as well as designing complex enterprise solutions in Java/JavaEE and Ruby. He started using Pentaho products from the very beginning (late 2003), gaining vast experience by deploying Pentaho as an open source, standalone BI solution. He also deeply integrated Pentaho as the analytics engine of choice in other applications he designed. Starting from 2009, based on his experience in the Java/JavaEE world and because of his appreciation for the open source world and its principles, he began participating actively as a contributor to some Pentaho projects, such as JPivot, Saiku, CDF, and CDA, and he has achieved the title of Pentaho Active Contributor.

In late 2010, he founded *Serasoft*, a young Italian consulting company specialized in the design and delivery of open source business intelligence solutions, and he started participating as a BI architect and Pentaho expert on a wide number of projects where open source BI and Pentaho were the main heroes. He is also the CTO of *Athilab* (*Athirat Innovation Lab*), sharing his experience in the design and delivery of high-value innovative enterprise solutions. He is always looking for innovative solutions that can help users make their work more efficient. He is also passionate about skiing, tennis, and photography.

About the Reviewer

Joel Latino was born in Ponte de Lima, Portugal, in 1989. He has been working in the IT industry since 2010, mostly as a software developer and BI developer.

He started his career at *Xpand-IT*—a Portuguese company specialized in strategic planning, consulting, implementation, and the maintenance of enterprise software that is fully adapted to the customer's needs—and earned his graduate degree in Informatics Engineering at the School of Technology and Management of the Viana do Castelo Polytechnic Institute.

Joel mainly focuses on open source web technology, databases, and business intelligence, and has some fascination with mobile technologies. He is responsible for developing some plugins to Pentaho Data Integration, such as Android and Apple push notification steps.

I would like to thank my parents for supporting me throughout my career and endeavors.

www.PacktPub.com

Support files, eBooks, discount offers and more

You might want to visit www.PacktPub.com for support files and downloads related to your book.

Did you know that Packt offers eBook versions of every book published, with PDF and ePub files available? You can upgrade to the eBook version at www.PacktPub.com and as a print book customer, you are entitled to a discount on the eBook copy. Get in touch with us at service@packtpub.com for more details.

At www.PacktPub.com, you can also read a collection of free technical articles, sign up for a range of free newsletters and receive exclusive discounts and offers on Packt books and eBooks.

http://PacktLib.PacktPub.com

Do you need instant solutions to your IT questions? PacktLib is Packt's online digital book library. Here, you can access, read and search across Packt's entire library of books.

Why Subscribe?

- ▸ Fully searchable across every book published by Packt
- ▸ Copy and paste, print and bookmark content
- ▸ On demand and accessible via web browser

Free Access for Packt account holders

If you have an account with Packt at www.PacktPub.com, you can use this to access PacktLib today and view nine entirely free books. Simply use your login credentials for immediate access.

Table of Contents

Preface

Pentaho Data Integration (PDI) is an ETL tool that was born 10 years ago. Its creator, Matt Caster, celebrated the 10th anniversary of this product, originally named Kettle (you can read the celebratory post on Matt's blog at: `http://www.ibridge.be/?p=211`), this year on March 8th 2013. The term K. E. T. T. L. E. is an acronym that stands for **Kettle Extraction Transformation Transport Load Environment**. When Pentaho acquired Kettle, its name was changed to Pentaho Data Integration, but actually, many developers continue to call it by the old name: Kettle.

How the story began...

The history of Kettle began in 2001 when Matt Caster, Pentaho Data Integration's chief architect and creator of Kettle, was working as a BI consultant. He had the idea of writing his own ETL tool to have a better and cheaper way to transfer data from one place to another. He was looking for a different solution, something that was better than inventing ugly data warehouse solutions written in PL/SQL, VB, or Shell scripts. He spent two years doing a thorough analysis of the problem. Because he was busy all the time with his work as a consultant, he worked on this project either during the weekends or at night. After this phase, he came out with a set of analyses documents and a couple of test programs written in C. He was not fully satisfied with what he got, so by early 2003, he started looking towards Java and continued his work on the product on this platform that, in those years, was gaining more traction in the market. So by the mid of 2003, the first version of the ETL design tool named Stir (which is now called Spoon) came to life.

It is interesting to see a screenshot of how things were then:

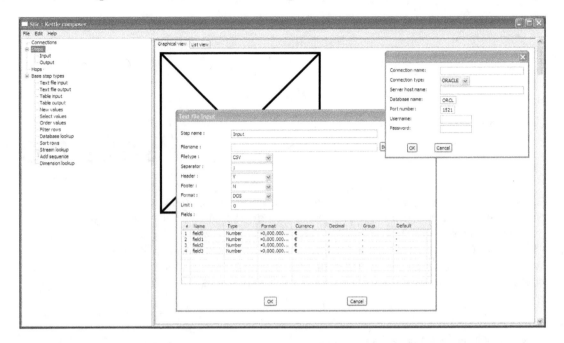

Stir featured a big X on the graphical view, and the log view was not working and neither were most step dialogs; but, it is useful for you to understand what the starting point of this adventure was. A certain number of other releases came out, each with a different set of new features or bugs fixed.

In 2004, work was reasonably stable and he was able to deploy Kettle for the first time to a customer. Because of the "real-world" situation, a lot of things needed to be fixed and new features needed to be implemented. That was why, in those days, things were advancing a lot faster than they were in the first three years. It seemed that the code base grew so fast that several refactorings and code cleanings were needed. Version 2.0 was one of the last "unstructured" versions. But it was thanks to the Java expertise from companies such as ixor (Wim De Clerq especially) that Kettle survived and changed radically. They helped Matt a lot with refactoring and code reorganizations to give the application a better structure and to simplify the code. At that time, Kettle had a fairly complete first release with support for slow-changing dimensions, junk dimensions, 28 steps, and 13 database connectors.

The application that was initially closed source was open sourced in late 2005. The first version under this new licensing mode was published in December 2005, and the response from the community was massive.

Kettle components

As of today, PDI is one of the best ETL open source solutions; it is made up of the following components:

- **Spoon**: This is a desktop application that uses a graphical interface and editor for transformations and jobs. It provides a way for you to create complex ETL jobs without having to read or write code. Any time you author, edit, run, or debug a transformation or job, you will use Spoon.

- **Pan**: This is a standalone command-line process that can be used to execute transformations and jobs created in Spoon.

- **Kitchen**: This is a standalone command-line process that can be used to execute jobs.

- **Carte**: Carte is a lightweight web container that allows you to set up a dedicated, remote ETL server.

What this book covers

Designing a simple PDI transformation (Simple) shows you how to design the simple transformation used as an example throughout all the recipes in this book. It also summarizes how we can develop a simple transformation using the design tool Spoon and some advises to follow in the development of transformations.

Designing a simple PDI job (Simple) shows you how to design a simple job that uses the transformation developed in the previous recipe. This job will be used as an example throughout all the book recipes. Like the previous recipe, it helps summarize how we can develop a simple job using the design tool Spoon and some advises to follow in the development of jobs and transformations.

Configuring command-line tools to run properly (Simple) represents the main starting point for everything. You will find what the main things are that you need to do to configure your PDI ETL system properly so that anything is able to work without any inconvenience.

Executing PDI jobs from a filesystem (Simple) is the first of a set of three recipes about how to start an ETL job from the command line. This is about how to start your PDI process when it is saved to the regular filesystem.

Executing PDI jobs packaged in archive files (Intermediate) explains the same topic as the previous recipe, but considers the process files to be packaged as an archive file. This is useful any time you use an ETL procedure on multiple systems (I mean for examples where you want to do some maintenance procedure) and you want to quickly move and run it without pain.

Executing PDI jobs from the repository (Simple) is the last in the series about how to start a job or transformation from the command line. This recipe is all about starting a job or transformation were the ETL files are stored in the repository.

Dealing with the execution log (Simple) explains how to efficiently use the various types of arguments available to manage the logfile and how to set the appropriate severity depending on the situation.

Discovering your PDI repository from the command line (Simple) is useful any time you decide to explore your PDI repository from the command line. It could so happen that you may forget what you have in your repository and where you have placed it. If that is the case, this is the recipe for you.

Exporting jobs and transformations to .zip files (Simple) shows you how to use a very simple and useful export mechanism. It could be useful to create a backup of your process files or to export them and easily move them to other systems.

Managing return code of PDI processes (Simple) is really the recipe for you if you need to get the procedure's return code to manage the conditional execution of other external processes.

Scheduling PDI jobs and transformations (Intermediate) tries to clear any doubts you have about scheduling your ETL processes.

What you need for this book

To run the samples in this book, you need a version of Java installed (JDK 1.6 or higher is fine) and you need the latest version of Pentaho Data Integration. If you don't have PDI installed, you can freely download it from this link: `http://kettle.pentaho.com`. For those of you who prefer to compile the version directly from the sources (I prefer to do this for my personal installation), you can get the latest sources from the following repository link: `svn://source.pentaho.org/svnkettleroot`.

Who this book is for

This book is for ETL developers with any amount of knowledge of PDI, from basic to advanced, and who already have knowledge about developing ETL processes using PDI. It is a book for anyone who wants to get a better idea about how to get their ETL processes running anywhere, manually or by scheduling, using command-line tools. You will have all the knowledge needed to do your work easily and without pain.

Conventions

In this book, you will find a number of styles of text that distinguish between different kinds of information. Here are some examples of these styles, and an explanation of their meaning.

Code words in text are shown as follows: "We can include other contexts through the use of the `include` directive".

A block of code is set as follows:

```
if "%PENTAHO_DI_JAVA_OPTIONS%"=="" set PENTAHO_DI_JAVA_OPTIONS=-
Xmx512m
```

Any command-line input or output is written as follows:

```
$ kitchen.sh -file:/home/sramazzina/tmp/samples/export-job.kjb
```

New terms and **important words** are shown in bold. Words that you see on the screen, in menus or dialog boxes for example, appear in the text like this: "Click on the **New** button from the toolbar menu".

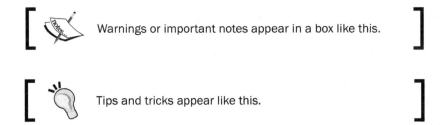

> Warnings or important notes appear in a box like this.

> Tips and tricks appear like this.

Reader feedback

Feedback from our readers is always welcome. Let us know what you think about this book—what you liked or may have disliked. Reader feedback is important for us to develop titles that you really get the most out of.

To send us general feedback, simply send an e-mail to feedback@packtpub.com, and mention the book title via the subject of your message.

If there is a topic that you have expertise in and you are interested in either writing or contributing to a book, see our author guide on www.packtpub.com/authors.

Customer support

Now that you are the proud owner of a Packt book, we have a number of things to help you to get the most from your purchase.

Downloading the example code

You can download the example code files for all Packt books you have purchased from your account at http://www.packtpub.com. If you purchased this book elsewhere, you can visit http://www.packtpub.com/support and register to have the files e-mailed directly to you.

Errata

Although we have taken every care to ensure the accuracy of our content, mistakes do happen. If you find a mistake in one of our books—maybe a mistake in the text or the code—we would be grateful if you would report this to us. By doing so, you can save other readers from frustration and help us improve subsequent versions of this book. If you find any errata, please report them by visiting `http://www.packtpub.com/submit-errata`, selecting your book, clicking on the **errata submission form** link, and entering the details of your errata. Once your errata are verified, your submission will be accepted and the errata will be uploaded on our website, or added to any list of existing errata, under the Errata section of that title. Any existing errata can be viewed by selecting your title from `http://www.packtpub.com/support`.

Piracy

Piracy of copyright material on the Internet is an ongoing problem across all media. At Packt, we take the protection of our copyright and licenses very seriously. If you come across any illegal copies of our works, in any form, on the Internet, please provide us with the location address or website name immediately so that we can pursue a remedy.

Please contact us at `copyright@packtpub.com` with a link to the suspected pirated material.

We appreciate your help in protecting our authors, and our ability to bring you valuable content.

Questions

You can contact us at `questions@packtpub.com` if you are having a problem with any aspect of the book, and we will do our best to address it.

Instant Pentaho Data Integration Kitchen

Welcome to Instant *Pentaho Data Integration Kitchen*. The aim of this book is to guide you in using the **Pentaho Data Integration** (**PDI**) command-line tools more effectively. It will help you in using **Kitchen** and **Pan** for your daily operations with PDI without any pain.

Designing a simple PDI transformation (Simple)

This recipe guides you through creating a simple **PDI transformation** using the graphical development environment **Spoon**. Using this simple example, we will see how to play with PDI command-line tools. The goal of this recipe is to extract a list of customers located in a selected country. The country to be exported is identified through an input parameter and the export is made to an Excel file located in the same directory where the transformation is run.

Getting ready

To get ready for this recipe, you first need to check that your Java environment is configured properly; to do this, check that the JAVA_HOME environment variable is set. Even if PDI while starting up tries to guess the value of the JAVA_HOME environment variable from the system, it is always good practice to set the JAVA_HOME environment variable. As soon as this is done, you need to start Spoon, the PDI's graphical development environment. You can start Spoon from the command line using the appropriate script located in the PDI's home directory. As soon as you get into the PDI home directory, you can run the proper script depending on the specific operating system environment.

Have a look at the following options:

▸ If you are on Windows, use the script `spoon.bat` to start the application

▸ If you are on Linux or Mac, use the script `spoon.sh` to start the application

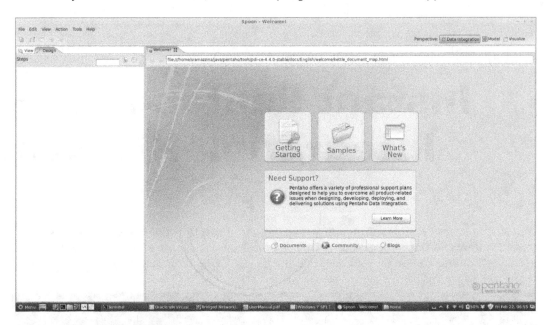

How to do it...

1. Create a new empty transformation. To do this, you can perform either of the following steps:

    1. Click on the **New** button from the toolbar menu and select the **Transformation** item entry.

    2. Select the **Transformation** item entry by navigating to **File | New** or by pressing *Ctrl + N*.

2. Go to the **Transformation properties** dialog and define a new transformation parameter called `p_country`. To do this, perform the following steps:

    1. Open the **Transformation settings** dialog by either pressing *Ctrl + T* or by right-clicking anywhere on the working area to the right and selecting **Transformation settings** from the newly displayed contextual menu.

2. Once the dialog opens, select the **Parameters** tab and add a new parameter called `p_country`.

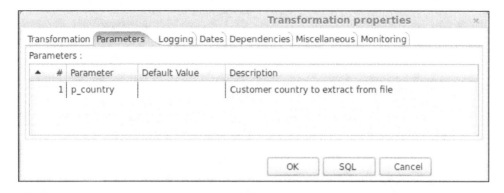

3. Select the **Design** tab from the left view. The list of category folders will appear in the **Steps** panel. Perform the following steps on them:

    1. From the **Input** category folder, get a **Text File Input** step and drag-and-drop it into the working area on the right.

    2. From the **Job** category folder, get a **Get Variables** step and drag-and-drop it into the working area on the right.

    3. From the **Flow** category folder, get a **Filter** and a **Dummy** step and drag-and-drop them into the working area on the right.

    4. Rename the **Dummy** step `Discarded customers`.

    5. From the **Output** category folder, get a **Microsoft Excel Output** step and drag-and-drop it into the working area on the right.

4. Connect the steps together in the following specified order:

    1. Connect the **Text File Input** step to the **Get Variable** step.

    2. Connect the **Get Variable** step to the **Filter** step.

    3. Connect the **Filter** step to the **Microsoft Excel Output** step and then connect the **Filter** step to the **Dummy** step as well.

5. Configure the **Text File Input** step as follows:

    1. Open the **Text File Input** step properties dialog by either double-clicking on the step icon in the working area or right-clicking on the step icon and selecting **Edit** step.

2. Configure the name of the step.

3. Under the **File** tab, configure the file to be read by typing the complete name of the file in the **File** or **Directory** input field. Because the sample file is located in the same sample directory where the transformation resides, a good approach to naming the file in a way that is location independent is to use a system variable to parameterize the directory name where the file is located. In our case, the complete filename is `${Internal.Transformation.Filename.Directory}/customers.txt`.

6. After the name of the file has been typed in, click on the **Add** button; the file will be added to the selected files located beneath as follows:

    1. Select the **Fields** tab. You must fill in the table describing the fields format.

    2. Click on the **Get Fields** button. The **Text File Input** step automatically analyzes a first set of 100 rows in the input file and tries to guess the field names to be imported. By the end of this inspection, all the fields will automatically get defined. Remember to verify the guessed data types so that only the `CUSTOMER_KEY` field has an Integer data type while the remaining fields have a String data type.

    3. Click on **OK** and close the **Text File Input** step properties dialog.

7. Configure the **Get Variable** step as follows:

    1. Open the **Get Variable** step properties by either double-clicking on the step icon in the working area or right-clicking on the step icon and selecting **Edit** step.

    2. Configure the name of the step.

    3. Click on the first row under the **Field** column, add a new column; named `filter_country` and press the *Tab* key.

    4. The cursor goes to the next column. Add the name of the parameter whose value is used to populate the new field: `${p_country}`. Press the *Tab* key.

    5. In the next column, where the cursor goes, select String as the data type of the new field.

    6. Click on **OK** and close the **Get Variable** step properties dialog.

8. Configure the **Filter** step as follows:

    1. Open the **Filter** step properties dialog by either double-clicking on the step icon in the working area or right-clicking on the step icon and selecting **Edit** step.

    2. From the **Send "true" data to** step combobox, select the **Write selected country customers** item entry to set the path that is to be navigated to any time the result of the condition is `true`.

3. From the **Send "false" data to** step combobox, select the **Discarded customers** item entry to set the path that is to be navigated to anytime the result of the condition is `false`.

4. Add a new condition called `COUNTRY = filter_country`.

5. To also manage the cases where the `p_country` parameter has not been set by the user, when starting the procedure, add another condition called `filter_country IS NULL`. Set this new condition as an alternate to the previous condition by using the `OR` logical operator.

6. Click on **OK** and close the **Filter** step properties dialog.

9. Configure the **Microsoft Excel Output** step as follows:

1. Open the **Microsoft Excel Output** step properties dialog by either double-clicking on the step icon in the working area or right-clicking on the step icon and selecting **Edit** step.

2. Configure the name of the step.

3. Under the **File** tab, configure the name of the export file by typing the complete name of the file in the **Filename** input field. Remember to write the name of the file without any extension because the file extension is located in the **Extension** input field. The exported file will be put in the same samples directory where the transformation resides. In any case, a good approach is to type the filename in a way that is location independent, using a system variable to parameterize the directory name where the file is located. In our case, the complete filename is `${Internal.Transformation.Filename.Directory}/selected_country_customers`.

4. Select the **Fields** tab. You must fill in the table describing the field's format.

5. Click on the **Get Fields** button. The **Text File Input** step automatically analyzes a first set of 100 rows in the input file and tries to guess the field names to be imported. At the end of this inspection, all the fields will automatically get defined.

6. Click on **OK** and close the **Microsoft Excel Output** step properties dialog.

10. Save the transformation with the suggested name `read-customers.ktr`.

11. The transformation design is now complete. You can now go to the *Design a simple job (Simple)* recipe and create the job that will use this transformation.

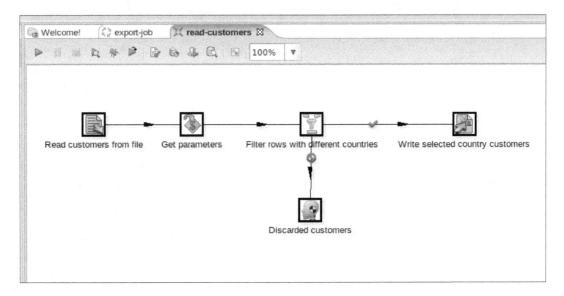

There's more...

Now that we have designed a sample transformation, let's analyze a quick way to easily find and get directly to the needed steps.

How to quickly find the steps to use

A set of category folders organizes transformations to facilitate the user's search process. If you are unsure about the right location of the step you are looking for, you can easily find it using the search functionality. To do this, go to the **Search** input text field located in the upper-left corner of the design view and write the name of the step you are looking for. While you are typing, you will see the items in the **Steps** panel whose name starts with the letters you are typing appear as shown in the following screenshot:

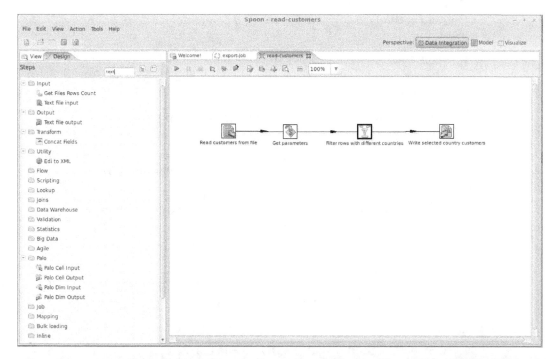

Designing a simple PDI job (Simple)

This recipe guides you through creating a simple **PDI job** using the graphical development environment Spoon. In a PDI process, jobs orchestrate other jobs and transformations in a coordinated way to realize our business process. This simple job uses the transformation created in the previous recipe, and we will use it as a simple example in this book's recipes, wherever necessary, to play with PDI command-line tools.

Getting ready

To get ready for this recipe, you need to check that the JAVA_HOME environment variable is set properly and then start the Spoon script. For more information on this, check what we detailed in the first recipe, *Designing a sample PDI transformation (Simple)*.

How to do it...

1. Create a new empty job. To do this, you can perform either of the following steps:
   - Click on the **New** button from the toolbar menu and select the **Job** item entry
   - Select the **Job** item entry by navigating to **File | New** or by pressing *Ctrl + ALT + N*.

2. Go to the **Job settings** dialog and define a new parameter called p_country. Do this as follows:

   1. Open the **Job settings** dialog by either pressing *Ctrl + J* or right-clicking on any place of the right working area and selecting **Job settings** from the newly displayed contextual menu.

3. Once the dialog opens, select the **Parameters** tab and add a new parameter called p_country.

4. Select the **Design** tab from the left-hand side view to display the list of tasks from their corresponding category folders. Look for the following tasks and drag-and-drop them into the working area on the right:

   1. From the **General** category folder, get a **Start** task and a **Transformation** task and drag-and-drop them into the working area.

   2. From the **File management** category folder, get a **Delete File** task and drag-and-drop it into the working area.

   3. From the **Utility** category folder, get an **Abort** task and drag-and-drop it into the working area on the right.

5. Connect the tasks together in the following specified order:

   1. Connect the **Start** task to the **Delete File** task.

   2. Connect the **Delete File** task to the **Transformation** task and then connect the **Delete File** task to the **Dummy** task as well.

   3. Connect the **Transformation** task to the **Success** task and then connect the **Transformation** task to the **Dummy** task as well.

   4. Connect the **Dummy** task to the **Abort** task.

6. Configure the **Delete File** task as follows:

   1. Open the **Delete File** task properties dialog by either double-clicking on the step icon in the working area or right-clicking on the step icon and selecting **Edit job entry**.

   2. Configure the name of the task.

   3. Configure the name of the file to be deleted by typing the complete name of the file in the **Filename** input field. The file to be deleted is located in the same samples directory where the transformation and the job reside. In any case, a good approach is to type the filename in a way that is location independent, using a system variable to parameterize the directory name where the file is located. In our case, the complete filename is ${Internal.Transformation.Filename.Directory}/selected_country_customers.xls.

4. As you can see in the **Properties** dialog, you can tick a checkbox so that the task will fail in case the file to be deleted does not exist.

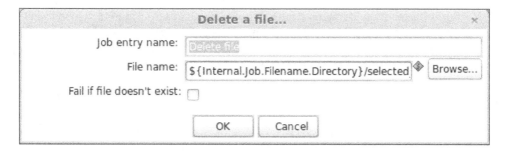

5. Click on **OK** and close the **Delete File** task properties dialog.

7. Configure the **Transformation** task as follows:

   1. Open the **Transformation** task properties dialog by either double-clicking on the step icon in the working area or right-clicking on the step icon and selecting **Edit job entry**.

   2. Configure the name of the task.

8. Under the **Transformation specification** tab, configure the name of the file for the transformation we're going to call. The transformation's file is located in the same samples directory where the job resides. In any case, a good approach is to type the filename in a way that is location independent, using a system variable to parameterize the directory name where the file is located. In our case, the complete filename is ${Internal.Job.Filename.Directory}/read-customers.ktr.

9. Save the job with the suggested name, export-job.kjb, in the same directory where you previously saved the transformation.

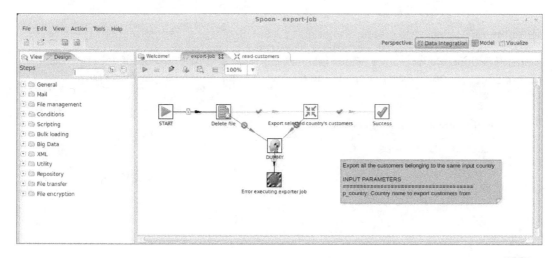

10. Try to execute the processes from the Spoon GUI. This is normally done by the developer to test or debug his/her jobs and transformations. To do this, click on the **Run** button, which can be identified by the green triangle icon located in the toolbar.

11. After the execution, if anything gets terminated successfully, the task icons will be decorated by a green mark that indicates that the specific tasks were executed successfully. Moreover, down in the working area, the **Job Entry** log details view indicates the results for every single task called by the job.

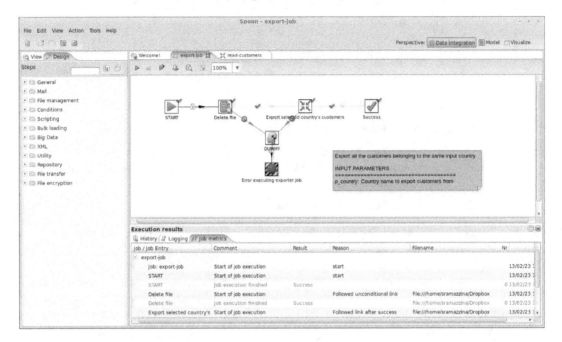

How it works...

A **Pentaho ETL** process is created generally by a set of jobs and transformations.

Transformations are workflows whose role is to perform actions on a flow of data by typically applying a set of basic action steps to the data. A transformation can be made by:

▶ A set of input steps

▶ A set of transformation steps

▶ A set of output steps

Input steps take data from external sources and bring them into the transformation. Examples of input steps are as follows:

- File input steps (text, Excel, properties, other)
- Table input steps
- OLAP source input steps or other similar steps

Transformation steps apply elementary business rules to the flow of data; the composition of this set of elementary transformation steps into an organized flow of operations represents a process. Examples of transformation steps are those that perform the following actions:

- Make operations on strings
- Make calculations
- Join different flow paths
- Apply scripts to the data with the goal of getting the results into other fields

Output steps send the data from the flow to external targets, such as databases, files, web services, or others. Therefore, we can say that transformations act as a sort of unit of work in the context of an entire ETL process. The more a transformation is atomic and concrete in its work, the more we can reuse it throughout other ETL processes.

Jobs are workflows whose role is to orchestrate the execution of a set of tasks: they generally synchronize and prioritize the execution of tasks and give an order of execution based on the success or failure of the execution of the current task. These tasks are basic tasks that either prepare the execution environment for other tasks that are next in the execution workflow or that manage the artifacts produced by tasks that are preceding them in the execution workflow. For example, we have tasks that let us manipulate the files and directories in the local filesystem, tasks that move files between remote servers through FTP or SSH, and tasks that check the availability of a table or the content of a table. Any job can call other jobs or transformations to design more complex processes. Therefore, generally speaking, jobs orchestrate the execution of jobs and transformations into large ETL processes.

In our case, we have a very simple example with a job and a transformation to support our recipes' experiments. The transformation gets data from a text file that contains a set of customers by country. After the data from the text file is loaded, it filters the dataflow by country and prints the result on an Excel file. The filter is made using a parameter that you set at the time you start the job and the filter step. The job checks if the previous file exists, and if so, deletes it and then calls the transformation for a new extraction. The job also has some failure paths to manage any sort of error condition that could occur during the processing of the tasks. The failure paths terminate with a step that aborts the job, marking it as failed.

There's more...

Every time we design a job or a transformation, there are some basic rules to follow to help you make things more easily portable between different systems, and, eventually, self-describing. The use of internal variables and a proper naming system for your job tasks and transformation steps are good rules of thumb. Then at the end, a brief recap of the various color and icon indicators that are implicitly present in the design of your process is also a good exercise. They help you to understand how the flow of information moves (inside your transformations) or how the set of operations execute in your flow (inside a job) quickly.

Why a proper naming for tasks and steps is so important

Each task in a job and each step in a transformation has a set of properties to let the user configure the expected behavior; one of these properties is used to give it a name. Giving tasks and steps an appropriate name is a very important thing because it helps us to make our transformations or jobs more readable. This suggestion becomes more valuable as the process becomes bigger. Documentation is always considered an unpleasant thing to do, but documenting processes is the only way to remember what we made, and why, in the long term. In this case, the correct naming of our components is something that, if done well, can be considered as a documentation in itself, at least for the insiders. And that is good enough!

Using internal variables to write location-independent processes

When writing our sample jobs and transformations, we used internal variables to set the path of the files we are reading or writing and set the path of the transformation file we have linked. This is very important to make our transformation and job location unaware so that we can easily move them here and there in our servers without any pain.

Kettle has two internal variables for this that you can access whenever required. By pressing *Ctrl + Space* directly from inside the field, you can activate the variables inspector to help you with finding out the right variable name without having to struggle with it. Going back to our problem of building a location-independent path, Kettle has two important system variables for this:

▶ **Internal.Job.Filename.Directory** – This is the directory name where the running job resides

▶ **Internal.Transformation.Filename.Directory** – This is the directory name where the running transformation resides

The important thing about these two variables is that PDI resolves them dynamically at runtime. So whenever you refer to a file, if you properly refer the path of the referred file to one of these two variables (depending on the case), you will be able to build location-unaware processes that will give you the ability to move them around without any pain.

The important role of icon and color indicators

Kettle jobs and transformations are full of visual indicators to help us easily and quickly understand why and when the flows follow this path, if the task or step is running, whether it's terminating successfully or not, or other such similar things. Taking care of these indications helps us a lot in understanding if everything has gone, or will go, according to what we intended.

Let's see some examples. While designing a transformation in Spoon, you can see that the connections between the steps (called **hops**) assume different colors or representation in different situations. The following screenshot shows a **Data Validator** step with a set of inputs and two outputs:

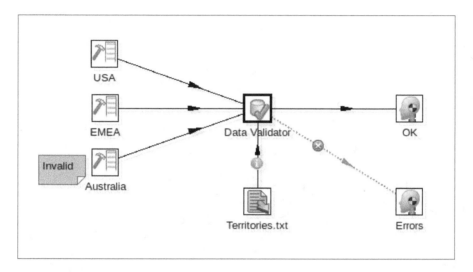

We can note two interesting things here:

1. One of the two output hops has been designed with a bold red dotted line, and this line has a red icon with an "x" sign on it. The red dotted line represents a path that carries the lines that caused an error. In this case, the error is related to the failure of the validation rule in the **Data Validator** step. The red "x" icon represents a graphical sign that enforces the information that this is an error path.

2. One of the input hops has a circular blue icon with a lowercase "i" character in it. This icon indicates that the hop connects a source step whose rows are an input to configure a parameter of the target step. In this case, the row that comes from the **Text File Input** step named **Territories.txt** configures a set of "allowed territories" that must be used to validate the rows that are coming in.

We can summarize the meaning behind the various hop colors as shown in the following table:

Color	Meaning
Green	The hop distributes rows; if multiple hops are leaving a step, rows of data will be distributed evenly to all the target steps
Red	The hop copies rows; if multiple hops are leaving a step, all rows of data will be copied to all the target steps
Yellow	The hop provides information for the step and distributes rows
Gray	The hop is disabled
Black	The hop has a named target step
Blue	Candidate hop using middle button and drag
Red (bold dotted line)	The hop is used for carrying rows that caused errors in the source step(s)

Other kinds of icons can be found while designing transformations in other situations. Let's see another example where a **Filter** step is going to be used:

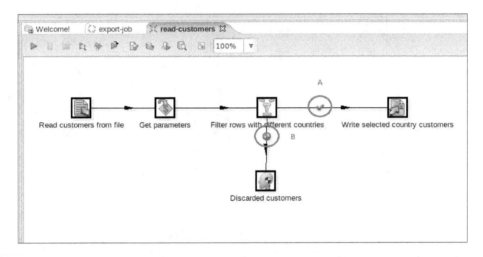

As you can see, the **Filter** step named **Filter rows with different countries** has two different output hops with two different icons indicated by the two red bold letters **A** and **B**:

> ▶ The icon indicated by the bold red letter **A** means that the hop is followed only when the condition specified in the **Filter** step has been satisfied (the result of the evaluation is true)

> ▶ The icon indicated by the bold red letter **B** means that the hop is followed only when the condition specified in the **Filter** step has not been satisfied (the result of the evaluation is false)

Similar concepts apply to a job's hops. Let's have a look at the following example:

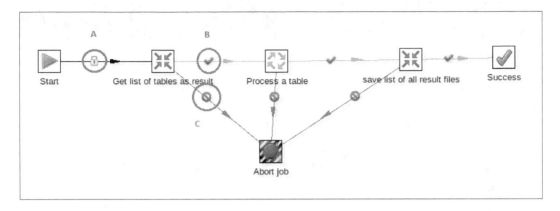

Because the jobs are process orchestrators in this case, a job hop is just an element of flow control. Hops link to job entries, and based on the results of the previous job entry, they determine what happens next. Icons help us to indicate the conditions under which that particular hop is followed:

- **Unconditional** – The icon identified by the red bold letter **A** in the screenshot represents this condition. It specifies that the next job entry will be executed regardless of the result of the originating job entry.

- **Follow when result is true** – The icon identified by the red bold letter **B** in the screenshot represents this condition. It specifies that the next job entry will be executed only when the result of the originating job entry is true.

- **Follow when result is false** – The icon identified by the red bold letter **C** in the screenshot represents this condition. It specifies that the next job entry will be executed only when the result of the originating job entry is false.

Again, hops in jobs assume different colors depending on the properties and the state of the job at that particular point:

- The hop connecting two tasks is *black* anytime the target entry is executed regardless of the result of the source entry (unconditional)

- The hop connecting two tasks is *green* anytime the target entry is executed if the result of the source entry is successful (result is true)

- The hop connecting two tasks is *black* anytime the target entry is executed if the result of the source entry is unsuccessful (result is false)

Configuring command-line tools to run properly (Simple)

This recipe guides you through configuring the script for command-line tools so that you can properly manage your execution performance in case of increased memory requirements. Many steps work in memory, so the more memory we reserve to PDI, coherently with the available memory and the overall system requirements, the better it is. A wrong memory configuration leads you to bad performance and/or unexpected `OutOfMemory` exception errors.

You will learn how to modify the script files Kitchen or Pan to set new memory requirements. This recipe will work the same for both Kitchen and Pan; the only difference to consider is in the names of the script files.

Getting ready

Remember that in PDI, we have two different sets of scripts to start PDI processes from the command line:

 ▶ The Kitchen scripts for starting PDI jobs
 ▶ The Pan scripts for starting PDI transformations

As soon as you get into the PDI home directory, you can edit them depending on the specific operating system environment.

So, let's move on and go to the PDI home directory and start working on this recipe.

How to do it...

To change the memory settings by modifying the script in Windows, perform the following steps:

1. From the PDI home directory, open the `kitchen.bat` (or `pan.bat`) script.

2. Scan through the script's code until you find the following lines of code:

    ```
    if "%PENTAHO_DI_JAVA_OPTIONS%"=="" set PENTAHO_DI_JAVA_OPTIONS=-Xmx512m
    ```

3. Change the value of the variable `PENTAHO_DI_JAVA_OPTIONS` to the required memory value for example, to `1024`:

    ```
    set PENTAHO_DI_JAVA_OPTIONS=-Xmx1024m
    ```

4. Save the file and exit.

To change the memory settings by modifying the script in Linux or Mac, perform the following steps:

1. From the PDI home directory, open the `kitchen.sh` script (or `pan.sh`).

2. Scan through the script's code until you find the following lines of code:

    ```
    if [ -z "$JAVAMAXMEM" ]; then
      JAVAMAXMEM="512"
    fi

    if [ -z "$PENTAHO_DI_JAVA_OPTIONS" ]; then
      PENTAHO_DI_JAVA_OPTIONS="-Xmx${JAVAMAXMEM}m"
    fi
    ```

3. Change the value of the variable `JAVAXMEM` to the required memory value for example, to `1024`:

    ```
    JAVAMAXMEM="1024"
    ```

4. Save the file and exit.

Downloading the example code

You can download the example code files for all Packt books you have purchased from your account at `http://www.packtpub.com`. If you purchased this book elsewhere, you can visit `http://www.packtpub.com/support` and register to have the files e-mailed directly to you.

Setting the environment variables in Windows is another, cleaner way to change the memory settings. To do this, you need to execute the steps summarized as follows:

1. Go to **Control Panel** and open the **Environment variables** dialog window.

2. Create a new system variable by clicking on the **New** button in the **System Environment Variable** section of the **Environment variables** dialog window.

3. Add a new variable called `PENTAHO_DI_JAVA_OPTIONS`.

4. Set the value of the variable. If we want to assign 1024 MB to PDI, for example, we set the variable's value to `-Xmx1024m`.

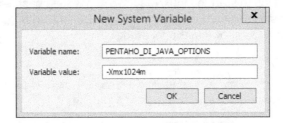

5. Click on **OK** to confirm and close the **New System Variable** dialog window.

6. Click on **OK** to close the **System Environment Variables** dialog window. This change will affect both scripts for jobs and transformations without any additional requirement.

To change the memory settings by setting the environment variables in Linux/Mac, perform the following steps:

1. Go to the **User** home directory and open the `.bash_profile` script file. If it does not exist, create a new one.

2. Add the following line to the script file:

   ```
   export PENTAHO_DI_JAVA_OPTIONS="-Xmx1024m"
   ```

3. Save and close the file. Remember that this new environment variable will either be visible in the user context starting from the next login or after closing and re-opening your terminal window.

There's more...

Setting the environment variable is a good way to configure our scripts seamlessly without modifying anything in the standard script. However, we can simplify our life by writing scripts that encapsulate all the internals related to the preparation of the script's execution environment. This lets us run our process without any hassle.

Making things easier by writing custom scripts

Kettle and Pan are two scripts that start our PDI processes from the command line. This means that they are full of switches that let us configure our PDI job to run properly. However, sometimes starting a job or a transformation is also a matter of preparing an execution environment that could require a bit of effort in terms of technical knowledge as well as a considerable amount of time. We do not usually want our user to be in such a situation. Therefore, to work around this, encapsulate the call to either the Kitchen or the Pan script, and the rest of the things will be taken care of by the custom script that does all of this without any pain.

Let's say we have a PDI job to start in Linux/Mac. We can write a bash script called `startMyJob.sh` that starts our job easily by configuring all the settings required to perform the job execution properly as shown in the following code:

```
#!/bin/bash

export PENTAHO_DI_JAVA_OPTIONS="-Xmx3072m -Djava.io.tmpdir=/mnt/tmp"
export KETTLE_HOME=/home/ubuntu/pdi_settings

/home/ubuntu/pentaho/data-integration/kitchen.sh -file=/home/
ubuntu/pentaho/etl/run_load.kjb -level=Basic -param:SKIP_FTP=false
-param:SKIP_DIMENSIONS=true "run_model"
```

As you can see, the code prepares the execution environment by setting the following:

- ▸ The memory options
- ▸ The location of a directory to store temporary files
- ▸ The KETTLE_HOME variable

Finally, it starts the PDI job. You can see how simple it is to start our job using this script instead of spending a lot of time on manual settings every time!

Executing PDI jobs from a filesystem (Simple)

This recipe guides you through simply starting a PDI job using the script Kitchen. In this case, the PDI job we are going to start is stored locally in the computer filesystem, but it could be anywhere in the network in any place that is directly accessible. You will learn how to start simple jobs both with and without a set of input parameters previously defined in the job.

Using command-line scripts is a fast way to start batches, but it is also the easiest way to schedule our jobs using our operating system's scheduler. The script accepts a set of inline arguments to pass the proper options required by the program to run our job in any specific situation.

Getting ready

To get ready for this recipe, we first need to check that our Java environment is configured properly; to do this, check that the JAVA_HOME environment variable is set. Even if all the PDI scripts, when started, call other scripts that try to find out about our Java execution environment to get the values of the JAVA_HOME variable, it is always a good rule of thumb to have that variable set properly anytime we work with a Java application.

The Kitchen script is in the PDI home directory, so the best thing to do to launch the script in the easiest way is to add the path to the PDI home directory to the PATH variable. This gives you the ability to start the Kitchen script from any place without specifying the absolute path to the Kitchen file location. If you do not do this, you will always have to specify the complete path to the Kitchen script file.

To play with this recipe, we will use the samples in the directory <book_samples>/sample1; here, <book_samples> is the directory where you unpacked all the samples of the book.

How to do it...

For starting a PDI job in Linux or Mac, use the following steps:

1. Open the command-line terminal and go to the <book_samples>/sample1 directory.

2. Let's start the sample job. To identify which job file needs to be started by Kitchen, we need to use the `-file` argument with the following syntax:

   ```
   -file: <complete_filename_to_job_file>
   ```

   Remember to specify either an absolute path or a relative path by properly setting the correct path to the file. The simplest way to start the job is with the following syntax:

   ```
   $ kitchen.sh -file:./export-job.kjb
   ```

3. If you're not positioned locally in the directory where the job files are located, you must specify the complete path to the job file as follows:

   ```
   $ kitchen.sh -file:/home/sramazzina/tmp/samples/export-job.kjb
   ```

4. Another option to start our job is to separately specify the name of the directory where the job file is located and then give the name of the job file. To do this, we need to use the `-dir` argument together with the `-file` argument. The `-dir` argument lets you specify the location of the job file directory using the following syntax:

   ```
   -dir: <complete_path_to_ job_file_directory>
   ```

   So, if we're located in the same directory where the job resides, to start the job, we can use the following new syntax:

   ```
   $ kitchen.sh - dir:. -file:export-job.kjb
   ```

5. If we're starting the job from a different directory than the directory where the job resides, we can use the absolute path and the `-dir` argument to set the job's directory as follows:

   ```
   $ kitchen.sh -dir:/home/sramazzina/tmp/samples -file:export-job.kjb
   ```

For starting a PDI job with parameters in Linux or Mac, perform the following steps:

1. Normally, PDI manages input parameters for the executing job. To set parameters using the command-line script, we need to use a proper argument. We use the `-param` argument to specify the parameters for the job we are going to launch. The syntax is as follows:

   ```
   -param: <parameter_name>= <parameter_value>
   ```

2. Our sample job and transformation does accept a sample parameter called `p_country` that specifies the name of the country we want to export the customers to a file. Let's suppose we are positioned in the same directory where the job file resides and we want to call our job to extract all the customers for the country U.S.A. In this case, we can call the Kitchen script using the following syntax:

   ```
   $ kitchen.sh -param:p_country=USA -file=./export-job.kjb
   ```

   Of course, you can apply the `-param` switch to all the other three cases we detailed previously.

For starting a PDI job in Windows, use the following steps:

1. In Windows, a PDI job from the filesystem can be started by following the same rules that we saw previously, using the same arguments in the same way. The only difference is in the way we specify the command-line arguments.

2. Any time we start the PDI jobs from Windows, we need to specify the arguments using the / character instead of the – character we used for Linux or Mac. Therefore, this means that:

   ```
   -file: <complete_filename_to_job_file>
   ```

   Will become:

   ```
   /file: <complete_filename_to_job_file>
   ```

   And:

   ```
   -dir: <complete_path_to_ job_file_directory>
   ```

   Will become:

   ```
   /dir: <complete_path_to_ job_file_directory>
   ```

3. From the directory <book_samples>/sample1, if you want to start the job, you can run the Kitchen script using the following syntax:

   ```
   C:\temp\samples>Kitchen.bat /file:./export-job.kjb
   ```

4. Regarding the use of PDI parameters in command-line arguments, the second important difference on Windows is that we need to substitute the = character in the parameter assignment syntax with the : character. Therefore, this means that:

   ```
   -param: <parameter_name>= <parameter_value>
   ```

   Will become:

   ```
   /param: <parameter_name>: <parameter_value>
   ```

5. From the directory <book_samples>/sample1, if you want to extract all the customers for the country U. S. A, you can start the job using the following syntax:

   ```
   C:\temp\samples>Kitchen.bat /param:p_country:USA /file:./export-job.kjb
   ```

For starting the PDI transformations, perform the following steps:

1. The Pan script starts PDI transformations. On Linux or Mac, you can find the pan.sh script in the PDI home directory. Assuming that you are in the same directory, <book_samples>/sample1, where the transformation is located, you can start a simple transformation with a command in the following way:

   ```
   $ pan.sh -file:./read-customers.ktr
   ```

2. If you want to start a transformation by specifying some parameters, you can use the following command:

    ```
    $ pan.sh –param:p_country=USA –file:./read-customers.ktr
    ```

3. In Windows, you can use the `Pan.bat` script, and the sample commands will be as follows:

    ```
    C:\temp\samples>Pan.bat /file:./read-customers.ktr
    ```

4. Again, if you want to start a transformation by specifying some parameters, you can use the following command:

    ```
    C:\temp\samples>Pan.bat /param:p_country=USA /file:./read-customers.ktr
    ```

Executing PDI jobs packaged in archive files (Intermediate)

This recipe guides you through starting a PDI job packed in an archived file (`.zip` or `.tar.gz`) using Kitchen. We will assume that the PDI job to be launched (we will call it the main job) and all the related jobs and transformations called during the execution are stored inside a `.zip` or `.tar.gz` archive file locally in the computer's filesystem; the execution will happen directly by accessing the files inside the archive without needing to unpack them to a local directory. This practice is a good idea in certain situations where we need to find a quick way to move our ETL processes around on different systems rapidly and without any pain; by packing everything in an archive file, we can move just one file instead of moving a bunch of files and directories—this really is easier!

Getting ready

To get ready for this recipe, you need to check that the JAVA_HOME environment variable is properly set and then configure your environment variables so that the Kitchen script can start from anywhere without specifying the complete path to your PDI home directory. For details about these checks, refer to the recipe *Executing PDI jobs from a filesystem (Simple)*.

To play with this recipe, you can use the samples in the directory <book_samples>/sample2; here, <book_samples> is the directory where you unpacked all the samples of the book.

How to do it...

For starting a PDI job from within a `.zip` or `.tar.gz` archive file in Linux or Mac, you can perform the following steps:

1. Open a command-line window and go to the <book_samples>/sample2 directory.

2. Kettle uses **Apache VFS** to let you access a set of files from inside an archive and use them directly in your processes; this is because it considers the archived content as a sort of **virtual filesystem** (**VFS**). To access a file in the archive, you need to give the complete path using a specific URI. In case you're going to access files contained in a `.zip` archive, the syntax to be used for the URI is as follows:

```
zip://arch-file-uri[!absolute-path]
```

On the other hand, if we wanted to access files contained in a `.tar.gz` file, we need to use the following syntax:

```
tgz://arch-file-uri[!absolute-path]
```

3. To identify which job file needs to be started, we need to use the `-file` argument with the following syntax; but now, the syntax has changed because we need to use, as a value, the URI with the syntax we saw in the preceding step:

```
-file: <complete_URI_to_job_file>
```

Remember that because we are talking about a URI to the file, we always need to consider the absolute path to the archive file followed by the path to the file we are going to start as a job.

4. To start the sample job named `export-job1.kjb` from within a `.zip` archive, use the following syntax:

```
$ kitchen.sh -file:'zip:///home/sramazzina/tmp/samples/samples.
zip!export-job1.kjb'
```

5. The usage of parameters from within the command-line tool is the same as we saw in the *Executing PDI jobs from a filesystem (Simple)* recipe. So, if we want to extract all the customers from the country U. S. A, the command to use is as follows:

```
kitchen.sh -param:p_country=USA -file:'zip:///home/sramazzina/tmp/
samples/samples.zip!export-job1.kjb'
```

6. Use the same command to start a job from within a `.tar.gz` archive, but with a different filesystem type in the URI. Here is a sample of a simple job that has been started without parameters:

```
$ kitchen.sh -file:'tgz:///home/sramazzina/tmp/samples/samples.
tar.gz!export-job1.kjb'
```

The following syntax is for a simple job that has been started with parameters:

```
kitchen.sh -param:p_country=USA -file:'tgz:///home/sramazzina/tmp/
samples/samples.tar.gz!export-job1.kjb'
```

7. Different from what we saw in the *Executing PDI jobs from a filesystem (Simple)* recipe, this time the `-dir` argument does not make any sense because we always need to access the archive through its complete URI and the `-file` argument.

For starting a PDI job from within a `.zip` archive file in Windows, perform the following steps:

1. Starting a PDI job from within an archive file on Windows requires for the same rules we saw previously to be followed using the same arguments in the same way.

2. Any time we start the PDI jobs from Windows, we need to specify the arguments using the / character instead of the – character we used in Linux or Mac. Therefore, this means that the `-file` argument will change from:

   ```
   -file: <complete_URI_to_job_file>
   ```

   To:

   ```
   /file: <complete_URI_to_job_file>
   ```

3. Go to the directory `<books_samples>/sample2`; to start your sample job from within the ZIP archive, you can start the Kitchen script using the following syntax:

   ```
   C:\temp\samples>Kitchen.bat /file:'zip:///home/sramazzina/tmp/
   samples/samples.zip!export-job1.kjb'
   ```

4. Let's create another example using parameters in the command. Go to the directory `<books_samples>/sample2`; to start the job by extracting all the customers for the country U. S. A, you can use the following syntax:

   ```
   C:\temp\samples>Kitchen.bat /param:p_country:USA /file:'zip:///
   home/sramazzina/tmp/samples/samples.zip!export-job1.kjb'
   ```

For starting PDI transformations from within archive files, perform the following steps:

1. PDI transformations are always started using Pan scripts. On Linux or Mac, you can find the `pan.sh` script in the PDI home directory. To start a simple transformation from within an archive file, go to the `<book_samples>/sample2` directory and type the following command:

   ```
   $ pan.sh -file: 'tgz:///home/sramazzina/tmp/samples/samples.tar.
   gz!export-job1.kjb'
   ```

   Or, if you need to specify some parameters, type the following command:

   ```
   $ pan.sh -param:p_country=USA -file:./read-customers.ktr
   ```

2. On Windows, you can use the `Pan.bat` script and the sample commands to start our transformation as follows:

   ```
   C:\temp\samples>Pan.bat /file='zip:///home/sramazzina/tmp/samples
   /samples.zip!read-customers1.ktr'
   ```

   Or, if you need to specify some parameters through the command line, type the following command:

   ```
   C:\temp\samples>Pan.bat /param:p_country:USA /file='zip:///home/
   sramazzina/tmp/samples/samples.zip!read-customers1.ktr'
   ```

How it works...

This way of starting jobs and transformations is possible because PDI uses the Apache VFS library to accomplish this task. The Apache VFS library is a piece of software that lets you directly access files from within any type of archive by exposing them through a virtual filesystem using an appropriate set of APIs. You can find more details about the library and how it works on the Apache website at `http://commons.apache.org/proper/commons-vfs`.

There's more...

Using jobs and transformations from within archive files slightly changes the way we design jobs and transformations. Another interesting consideration is that you can directly reference resource files packed together with your ETL process file. This lets you distribute configuration files or other kinds of resources in a uniform way. This approach could be an easy way to have a single file containing anything needed by our ETL process, making everything more portable and easier to manage. The following paragraph details the main changes applied to this new version of our sample.

Changes in job and transformation design

When jobs or transformations are used from inside an archive, the files relate to the root of the archive, and the internal variable `${Internal.Job.Filename.Directory}` does not make any sense. Because of this, we need to change the way our example process links any kind of file.

Look at the samples located in the directory `<book_samples>/sample2`; this directory contains the same transformations and jobs, but they need to undergo major changes for them to work in this case. They are as follows:

- ▸ The job links the transformation without using the system variable `${Internal.Job.Filename.Directory}` to dynamically obtain the path to the job file. This is because, internally to the archive file, the transformation is in the root of this virtual filesystem, so the filename is enough for this purpose.

- ▸ Instead of using the `${Internal.Job.Filename.Directory}` variable to specify the input and output path for the files, we added two new parameters, `p_input_directory` and `p_target_directory`, to let the user specify the input directory and output directory. If we have not specified a value for these parameters, we'll set a default value that is local to the directory where the job starts.

Executing PDI jobs from the repository (Simple)

This recipe guides you through starting PDI jobs using Kitchen by assuming that PDI jobs are stored in the PDI repository. We will learn how to start simple jobs both with and without a set of input parameters previously defined in the job.

There are different versions of repositories that you can use depending on your needs: filesystem, database, and Pentaho repository.

- The **filesystem repository** is a very easy form of repository; it lets you store your files at a specified location in the filesystem.
- The **database repository** is another simple form repository that uses database tables as a way to have a unique central objects store. It is usually an authenticated repository and does not have any kind of versioning or locking mechanism on the object, so it is not recommended for team development.
- The last type of repository, the **Pentaho repository**, is a sophisticated repository environment for safely storing our BI object (and so our ETL processes) available only for the Enterprise Edition (EE) of PDI.

Getting ready

To play with this recipe, I prepared a filesystem repository in the `<book_samples>/sample3` directory with all the related transformations and the job in it. The repository is located in the `samples/sample3` directory. To have our example working fully, we need to add the filesystem repository (see the *How to define a filesystem repository* section under the *There's more...* section of this recipe for details about it) to PDI by specifying the complete path to the `<book_samples>/sample3` directory in the base directory field.

Check if the `JAVA_HOME` environment variable is set properly and configure your environment variables so that the Kitchen script can start from anywhere without specifying the complete path to your PDI home directory. For details about these checks, refer to the *Executing PDI jobs from a filesystem (Simple)* recipe.

How to do it...

For starting a PDI job from a filesystem repository in Linux or Mac, perform the following steps:

1. Let's start our sample job from the repository; to do this, we need to use two new arguments:
   - The `-rep` argument identifies the repository we are going to connect to; the syntax is as follows:

     ```
     -rep: <id_of_the_repository>
     ```

❑ The -job argument specifies the name of the job that needs to be started; the syntax is as follows:

```
-job: <name_of_the_job>
```

2. So, because the ID of our repository is `sample3`, we'll start the sample job with the following syntax:

```
$ kitchen.sh -rep:sample3 -job: export-job
```

3. Suppose that the job is not located in the root directory of our repository, but is stored in the `pdi_book` directory; to start it, we must specify the correct path to the job in the repository with the following syntax using the -dir argument:

```
$ kitchen.sh -rep:sample3 -dir:/pdi_book  -job:export-job
```

4. Parameter usage from within the command-line tool is exactly the same as we saw in the previous recipes. So, if we want to extract all the customers from the country U.S.A, a sample of the command to use is as follows:

```
kitchen.sh -param:p_country=USA --rep:sample3 -job: export-job
```

For starting a PDI job from a filesystem repository on Windows, perform the following steps:

1. Starting a PDI job from within a filesystem repository on Windows requires for the same rules we saw previously to be followed with the exception that, as usual, we need to specify the arguments using the / character instead of the - character that we used for Linux or Mac. So, the -rep argument will change to /rep:

```
/rep: < id_of_the_repository >
```

And the -job argument will change to /job:

```
/job: < name_of_the_job >
```

2. Let's suppose that the job is located in the root directory of our repository; we can call the Kitchen script using the following syntax:

```
C:\temp\samples>Kitchen.bat /rep:sample3 /job:export-job
```

3. About the use of PDI parameters through the command-line arguments: let's suppose we run our job by extracting all the customers for the country U.S.A; we can call our job using the following syntax:

```
C:\temp\samples>Kitchen.bat /rep:sample3 /job:export-job /
param:p_country:USA
```

For starting a PDI job from a database repository, perform the following steps:

1. The process of starting a PDI job in a database repository is the same as in a filesystem repository. The only difference in this case is that a database repository is an authenticated source, so it requires a username and password.

2. The `-user` parameter lets you specify a valid username to connect to the repository. If you are on Linux/Mac, the syntax will be as follows:

```
-user: <repository_username>
```

3. For Windows, you need to change the – character to the / character; the syntax is as follows:

```
/user: <repository_username>
```

4. The `-pass` argument lets you specify a valid password for the user you are using to connect to the database repository; the syntax in this case for Linux/Mac is as follows:

```
-pass: <repository_user_password>
```

And for Windows, the syntax is as follows:

```
/pass: <repository_username>
```

5. Suppose that our job, called `export-job.kjb`, is located in a database repository instead of in a filesystem repository, and that we are connecting to the user `pdiuser` with the password `password`. The example command to start the job in Linux/Mac is as follows:

```
$ kitchen.sh -user:pdiuser -pass:password -rep:sample3 -dir:/pdi_
book   -job:export-job
```

Whereas in Windows, the syntax is as follows:

```
C:\temp\samples>Kitchen.bat /user:pdiuser /pass:password /
rep:sample3 /job:export-job
```

There's more...

Up until now, we worked with jobs and transformations saved as XML files in the plain filesystem. Let's discuss some important things in the following sections that will help them work properly if we were to store them in a repository. Then, we'll talk about how to define a filesystem and a database repository.

Changes in job and transformation design

When using jobs and transformations from within repositories (either database or files), things change slightly. In this case, the ETL process files relate to the root of the repository, and the internal variable `Internal.Job.Filename.Directory` does not make any sense. Because of this, we need to change the way our example job links jobs or transformations or any kind of file. The major changes are as follows:

- The job links the transformation using the system variable `Internal.Job.Repository.Directory` to dynamically get the path to the job file in the repository. This system variable gives you the path to the job file being executed in the repository at runtime.

- To specify the input and output path for all the files read or written from or to the outside world, we added two new parameters, `p_input_directory` and `p_target_directory`, to specify the absolute or relative path (it depends on your needs) to the input and output directories. In our examples, these parameters default to the local directory where the job or transformation starts.

How to define a filesystem repository

Creating a filesystem repository is a fairly easy task. Let's follow the ensuing summarized steps and try to define a new one:

1. Start Spoon and navigate to **Tools** | **Repository** | **Connect**. The repository connection dialog opens.

2. Click on the new repository button (the green circular button with the **+** icon in it). The **Select repository type** dialog box opens.

3. Spoon lets you decide between the two repository types. Choose the filesystem repository type and click on **OK**. The **File repository settings** dialog box opens in front of you.

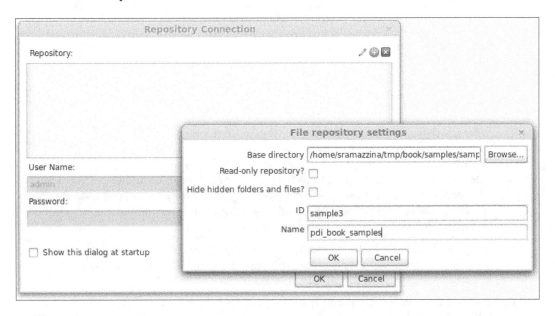

4. Select the base directory that will contain the repository objects (in our case, it is the `<book_samples>/sample3` directory).

5. Fill in the **ID** field with the ID of the repository; in our case, the ID of the repository is `sample3`.

6. Set a name for the repository. You can even use spaces in your repository name because it is just a sort of label.

7. Click on **OK** and you are done. The newly created repository will appear in the list of available repositories.

Defining a database repository

The process to define a database repository is almost identical to what we saw in the previous paragraph regarding the filesystem repository. The difference here is that PDI requires a connection definition where it can create the related repository's database tables. Let's follow the ensuing summarized steps to create a new one:

1. Start Spoon and navigate to **Tools | Repository | Connect**. The repository connection dialog opens.

2. Click on the new repository button (the green circular button with the **+** icon in it). The **Select repository type** dialog box opens.

3. Spoon lets you decide between the two repository types. Choose the database repository type and click on **OK**. The **Repository information** dialog box opens in front of you.

4. Choose the connection name from a list of connections. In case there is no valid connection to use, you can define it by clicking on the **New** button (we assume you already know how to define a connection and that you already have a connection available). Fill in the repository ID and repository name.

5. If you don't have an existing repository or if you are accessing an old repository version, you can respectively create the necessary tables or upgrade the existing ones by clicking on the **Create or Upgrade** button.

6. Click on **OK** and you are done. The newly created repository will appear in the list of available repositories.

Dealing with the execution log (Simple)

This recipe guides you through managing the PDI execution log in terms of the following aspects:

- ► Setting up the verbosity level
- ► Redirecting it to an output file for future reference

This recipe will work the same for both Kitchen and Pan; the only difference is in the name of the script's file used to start the process.

Getting ready

To get ready for this recipe, you need to check that the JAVA_HOME environment variable is properly set and then configure your environment variables so that the Kitchen script can start from anywhere without specifying the complete path to your PDI home directory. For details about these checks, refer to the recipe *Executing PDI jobs from a filesystem (Simple)*.

How to do it...

For changing the log's verbosity level, perform the following steps:

1. Open a command-line window and go to the `<book_samples>/sample1` directory.

2. Any time that we are going to start a job or a transformation, we can manually set the verbosity of our log output. The more verbosity you choose to have, the more logs will be produced. To do this, we can use the `-level` argument specified for Linux/Mac as follows:

   `-level: <logging_level>`

   And for Windows, the argument specified is as follows:

   `/level: <logging_level>`

3. The `-level` argument lets you specify the desired logging level by choosing its value from a set of seven possible values specified as follows:

   - ❑ `Error`: This level is intended only to show errors
   - ❑ `Nothing`: This means the argument isn't showing any output
   - ❑ `Minimal`: This level uses minimal logging and provides a low verbosity on your log output
   - ❑ `Basic`: This is the default basic logging level
   - ❑ `Detailed`: This is intended to be used as soon as you require a detailed logging output

❑   Debug: This is used for debugging purposes for a very detailed output

❑   Rowlevel: The maximum amount of verbosity; logging at a row level can generate a lot of data

4. To start the job in Linux/Mac with a log level set to the Error level, we can give the following command:

```
$ kitchen.sh -file:/home/sramazzina/tmp/samples/export-job.
kjb -level:Error
```

5. To start the job in Windows with a log level set to the Error level, we can give the following command:

```
C:\temp\samples>Kitchen.bat /file C:\temp\samples\export-job.kjb /
level:Error
```

For saving an ETL process log to output files for future reference, use the following steps:

1. The log produced by our Kettle processes is an invaluable resource to properly diagnose problems and solve them quickly. So, it is a good rule of thumb to save the logs and eventually archive them for future reference.

2. In case you are launching your jobs from the command line, there are different ways to save the log.

3. The first thing we can do is save the log to a file using the `logfile` argument. This argument lets you specify the complete path to the logfile name.

4. To set the logfile name on Linux/Mac, use the following syntax:

```
-logfile: <complete_logfilename>
```

5. To set the logfile name on Windows, use the following syntax:

```
/logfile: <complete_logfilename>
```

6. Let 's suppose that we are going to start the `export-job.kjb` Kettle job, and we want a Debug log level and to save the output to a specified logfile called `pdilog_debug_output.log`. To do this on Linux/Mac, type the following command:

```
$ kitchen.sh -file:/home/sramazzina/tmp/samples/export-job.
kjb -level:Debug -logfile:./pdilog_debug_output.log
```

7. To set the logfile on Windows, type the following command:

```
C:\temp\samples>Kitchen.bat /file:C:\temp\samples\export-job.kjb /
level:Debug /logfile:.\pdiloc_debug_output.log
```

8. As soon as your PDI starts, it will start filling a buffer that contains all the rows produced by your log. This is interesting because it lets you keep the memory usage under control. By default, PDI maintains the first 5000 logs' rows produced by your job in this buffer. This means that if your ETL process produces more than 5000 rows, the output log is truncated.

9. To change the length of the log buffer, you need to use the `maxloglines` argument; this argument lets you specify the maximum number of log lines.

10. To set the maximum number of log lines that are kept by Kettle on Linux/Mac, use the following argument:

    ```
    -maxloglines: <number_of_log_lines_to_keep>
    ```

11. To set the maximum number of log lines that are kept by Kettle on Windows, use the following argument:

    ```
    /maxloglines: <number_of_log_lines_to_keep>
    ```

12. If you specify 0 as the value for this argument, PDI will maintain all of the log lines produced.

13. Another method to limit the number of log lines kept internally by the PDI logging system is to filter log lines by age. The `maxlogtimeout` argument lets you specify the maximum age of a log line in minutes before it is removed by the log buffer.

14. To set the maximum age of a log line on Linux/Mac in minutes, use the following argument:

    ```
    -maxlogtimeout: <age_of_a_logline_in_minutes>
    ```

15. To set the maximum age of a log line on Windows in minutes, use the following argument:

    ```
    /maxlogtimeout: <age_of_a_logline_in_minutes>
    ```

16. If you specify 0 as the value for this argument, PDI will maintain all the log lines indefinitely.

17. Let's suppose, for example, that we're going to start the `export-job.kjb` Kettle job and that we want to keep 10000 rows in our log buffer. In this case, the command we need to use in Linux/Mac is as follows:

    ```
    $ kitchen.sh -file:/home/sramazzina/tmp/samples/export-job.kjb -
    level:Debug -logfile:./pdilog_debug_output.log -maxloglines:10000
    ```

There's more...

The log is an invaluable source of information that is useful to understand what and where something does not work. This will be the topic covered by the first paragraph of this section. Then, we will see a brief example that helps us produce logfiles with a parametric name.

Understanding the log to identify where our process fails

The log that our ETL process produces contains a valuable set of information that helps us understand where our process fails. The first case of failure is given by a system exception. In this case, it is very easy to identify why our process fails because the exception message is clearly identifiable in the logfile. As an example, let's suppose that we're starting our job from a wrong directory or that our job file is not found in the path we're giving; we will find a detailed exception message in the log as follows:

```
INFO  17-03 22:15:40,312 - Kitchen - Start of run.

ERROR: Kitchen can't continue because the job couldn't be loaded.
```

However, a very different thing is when our process does not explicitly fail because of an exception, but the results are different from what is expected. It could be that we expected 1000 rows to be written to our file, but only 900 were written. Therefore, what can we do to understand what is going wrong? A simple but effective way to try to understand what goes wrong is to analyze an important part of our log that summarizes what happened for each of our tasks. Let's consider the following section taken from the log of one of our sample processes:

```
INFO  17-03 22:31:54,712 - Read customers from file - Finished processing
(I=123, O=0, R=0, W=122, U=1, E=0)

INFO  17-03 22:31:54,720 - Get parameters - Finished processing (I=0,
O=0, R=122, W=122, U=0, E=0)

INFO  17-03 22:31:54,730 - Filter rows with different countries -
Finished processing (I=0, O=0, R=122, W=122, U=0, E=0)

INFO  17-03 22:31:54,914 - Write selected country customers - Finished
processing (I=0, O=122, R=122, W=122, U=0, E=0)
```

As you can clearly see, the section that can always be found almost at the end of any transformation called by the job summarizes what happens at the boundaries (input and output) of every step of our transformation. Keeping an eye on this log fragment is a key point in understanding where our business rules are failing and where we are getting lesser records than expected. On the other hand, remember that because jobs are mainly orchestrators, they do not contain any data, so there is no need for such a log section for them.

Separating execution logfiles by date and time

It could be interesting to separate our execution logs by appending the execution date and time to the logfile name. To do this, the simplest thing we can do is to wrap our Kitchen script in another script used to set the proper logfile name using some shell functions.

As an example, I wrote a sample script for Linux/Mac that starts PDI jobs by filename and writes a logfile whose name is made up of a base name, a text string containing the date and time when the job was submitted, and the extension (conventionally .log). Have a look at the following code:

```
now=$(date +"%Y%m%d_%H%M%s")
kitchen.sh -file:$1.kjb -logfile:$2_$now.log
```

As you can see, it's a fairly trivial script; the first line builds a string composed by year, month, name, hour, minutes, and seconds, and the second concatenates that string with a logfile's base name and extension. To start the script, use the following syntax:

```
startKitchen.sh <job_to_start_base_name> <logfile_base_name>
```

So, for example, the following command starts Kitchen by calling the job export-job.kjb and produces a logfile called logfile_20130319_13261363696006.log:

```
$./startKitchen.sh ./export-job ./logfile
```

You can do a similar batch for the Windows platform.

Discovering your PDI repository from the command line (Simple)

This recipe guides you through discovering the structure and content of your PDI repository using the PDI command-line tools. We can know anything about the repository from the command line: we can view the list of available repositories, or view the list of directories in the repository, view the list of jobs or transformations in the specified directory. This recipe will work the same for both Kitchen and Pan, with the exception of the listing of jobs and transformations in a repository's directory; the first works with Kitchen and the second with Pan.

Getting ready

To get ready for this recipe, you need to check that the JAVA_HOME environment variable is set properly and then configure your environment variables so that the Kitchen script can start from anywhere without specifying the complete path to your PDI home directory. For details about these checks, refer to the recipe *Executing PDI jobs from a filesystem (Simple)*.

How to do it...

To get the list of the available repositories, perform the following steps:

1. Sometimes we need to start a job or a transformation but we do not have the details of the repository we are going to interact with. The first thing we need to know is the name of the repository we are going to connect to to start our process. To get the name of the available repositories, we can use the `listrep` command-line argument.

2. The usage is very simple because it does not need any value, just the name of the argument specified in the command line.

3. Imagine that we need to find the list of the available repositories on Linux/Mac; the command to give is as follows:

   ```
   $ kitchen.sh -listrep
   ```

4. To do the same thing on Windows, the command is written as follows:

   ```
   C:\temp\samples>Kitchen.bat /listrep
   ```

5. The result we get is the repositories listed in a clear and concise form with the repository ID in the first column and the repository name in the second column:

   ```
   INFO  19-03 23:18:51,675 - Kitchen - Start of run.

   INFO  19-03 23:18:51,695 - RepositoriesMeta - Reading repositories
   XML file: /home/sramazzina/.kettle/repositories.xml

   List of repositories:

   #1 : sample3 [PDI Book Samples]  id=KettleFileRepository
   ```

To get the list of directories in a selected repository, perform the following steps:

1. The next step after we have found the repository we were looking for could be to look for a job or transformation located somewhere in the repository.

2. To do this, we need to get the list of available directories in the repository using the `listdir` argument used together with the following arguments:

   - The `rep` argument, to specify the name of the repository where we want to display the internal directory structure.

   - The `dir` argument, to give the directory name's starting point. The command will show you the directories contained in a specific directory. If this argument has not been specified, PDI assumes that you want to show all the directories contained in the root directory. Navigating through the structure of a complex repository is quite a tedious and iterative process, but something is better than nothing!

   - The `user` and `-pass` arguments, in case your repository is an authenticated repository, to specify the username and password that needs to be connected to.

3. To find the list of the available directories in the root of the repository `rep3`, the command to fire on Linux/Mac is as follows:

   ```
   $ kitchen.sh -rep:sample3 -listdir
   ```

4. To find the list of the available directories in the root of the repository `rep3`, the command to fire on Windows is as follows:

   ```
   C:\temp\samples>Kitchen.bat /rep:sample3 /listdir
   ```

5. The command returns the list of available directories in the following form:

   ```
   INFO   20-03 07:07:17,236 - Kitchen - Start of run.
   INFO   20-03 07:07:17,252 - RepositoriesMeta - Reading repositories
   XML file: /home/sramazzina/.kettle/repositories.xml
   dir2
   dir1
   ```

6. The directory `dir1` has a subdirectory, `subdir11`; to show this directory, we need to specify another command that for Linux/Mac is as follows:

   ```
   $ kitchen.sh -rep:sample3 -dir:dir1 -listdir
   ```

   And for Windows, the command is as follows:

   ```
   C:\temp\samples>Kitchen.bat /rep:sample3 /dir:dir1 /listdir
   ```

7. PDI will show us the children of the directory `dir1` as follows:

   ```
   INFO   20-03 07:07:34,324 - Kitchen - Start of run.
   INFO   20-03 07:07:34,339 - RepositoriesMeta - Reading repositories
   XML file: /home/sramazzina/.kettle/repositories.xml
   subdir11
   ```

8. If you're checking the directories of an authenticated repository, the command will change as follows for Linux/Mac:

   ```
   $ kitchen.sh -user:pdiuser -pass:password -rep:sample3 -listdir
   ```

   And the command will change as follows for Windows:

   ```
   C:\temp\samples>Kitchen.bat /user:pdiuser /pass:password /
   rep:sample3 /listdir
   ```

9. The output of the command will remain the same.

To get the list of jobs in a specified directory, perform the following steps:

1. Now that we know about the internals of our repository, we're ready to look for our jobs.

2. The argument used to show the list of the available jobs in a specified directory is `listjob`. This argument must be used together with the following:

   ❑ The `rep` argument, to specify the name of the repository where we want to display the internal directory structure.

   ❑ The `dir` argument, to give the name of the directory. The command will show you the jobs contained in a specific directory. If this argument is not specified, PDI assumes that you want to show all the jobs contained in the root directory.

   ❑ The `user` and `pass` arguments, in case your repository is an authenticated repository, to specify the username and password that needs to be connected to.

3. To find the list of the available jobs in the root directory of the repository `rep3`, the command to fire on Linux/Mac is as follows:

   ```
   $ kitchen.sh -rep:sample3 -listjobs
   ```

4. To find the list of the available jobs in the root directory of the repository `rep3`, the command to fire on Windows is as follows:

   ```
   C:\temp\samples>Kitchen.bat /rep:sample3 /listjobs
   ```

5. The command returns the list of available jobs in the following form:

   ```
   INFO  20-03 07:30:46,642 - Kitchen - Start of run.

   INFO  20-03 07:30:46,657 - RepositoriesMeta - Reading repositories
   XML file: /home/sramazzina/.kettle/repositories.xml

   export-job
   ```

6. If you're checking the jobs in an authenticated repository, the command on Linux/Mac will change in the following way:

   ```
   $ kitchen.sh -user:pdiuser -pass:password -rep:sample3 -listjobs
   ```

7. If you're checking the jobs in an authenticated repository, the command on a Windows platform will change in the following way:

   ```
   C:\temp\samples>Kitchen.bat /user:pdiuser /pass:password /
   rep:sample3 /listjobs
   ```

To get the list of transformations in a specified directory, perform the following steps:

1. The Pan script lets us see the list of transformations contained in a directory of our repository.

2. To do this, we need to specify the `-listtrans` argument together with the same arguments specified for the `-listjobs` argument; for details about this, please refer to the previous paragraph to get a detailed explanation of the meaning and syntax of those arguments.

3. To find the list of the available transformations in the root directory of the repository `rep3`, the command to fire on Linux/Mac is as follows:

```
$ pan.sh -rep:sample3 -listtrans
```

4. To find the list of the available transformations in the root directory of the repository `rep3`, the command to fire on Windows is as follows:

```
C:\temp\samples>Pan.bat /rep:sample3 /listtrans
```

5. The command returns the list of available transformations in the following form:

```
INFO   20-03 07:35:10,073 - Pan - Start of run.

INFO   20-03 07:35:10,103 - RepositoriesMeta - Reading repositories
XML file: /home/sramazzina/.kettle/repositories.xml

read-customers
```

6. Anything applied to the display of jobs contained in a specific directory and the ability to apply the same command to an authenticated repository applies here to transformations as well; the only recommendation is to remember to use the Pan script instead of the Kitchen script.

Exporting jobs and transformations to the .zip files (Simple)

This recipe guides you through exporting the structure and content of your PDI repository using the PDI command-line tools. The first trivial use of this option is for something such as the backup of our job. The job and all of its dependencies will be exported to a ZIP file that we can, for example, move to another location for archiving. But at the end, what's the funny part of all of this? The job that you exported in your `.zip` archive starts directly from the exported archive file. For details about how to start a job from an archive file, follow what we explained in the recipe *Executing PDI jobs packaged in archive files (Intermediate)*. This recipe will work the same for both Kitchen and Pan.

Getting ready

To get ready for this recipe, you need to check that the JAVA_HOME environment variable is set properly and then configure your environment variables so that the Kitchen script can start from anywhere without specifying the complete path to your PDI home directory. For details about these checks, refer to the recipe *Executing PDI jobs from a filesystem (Simple)*.

How to do it...

To dump the jobs stored in a PDI repository to an archive file, use the following steps:

1. Dumping a job stored in a repository, either authenticated or not, is an easy thing. To try the following examples, use the filesystem repository we defined during the recipe *Executing PDI jobs from the repository (Simple)*.

2. To export a job and all of its dependencies, we need to use the export argument followed by the base name of the .zip archive file that we want to create. Remember that you don't need to specify any extension for the exported file because it will get attached automatically.

3. This kind of repository is unauthenticated, but you can do exactly the same things using an authenticated repository by specifying the username and password to connect to the repository.

4. To export the job export-job from the samples3 repository on Linux/Mac, type the following command:

   ```
   $ kitchen.sh -rep:sample3 -job:export-job -export:sample-export
   ```

5. To export the job export-job from the samples3 repository on Windows, type the following command:

   ```
   C:\temp\samples>Kitchen.bat /rep:sample3 /job:export-job /
   export:sample-export
   ```

To dump the jobs stored in the filesystem to an archive file, use the following steps:

1. You can do the same things to export jobs stored in the plain filesystem; in this case, the job must specify the files related to the job that is to be exported:

   - Using the file argument and giving the complete path to the job file in the filesystem
   - Using the file and dir arguments together

2. For details about the usage of these arguments, see the recipe *Executing PDI jobs from a filesystem (Simple)*. Let's go to the directory <books_samples>/sample1.

3. To try to export all of the files related to the export-job.kjb job in Windows, type the following command:

   ```
   kitchen.sh -file:./export-job.kjb -export:sample-export
   ```

4. To try to export all of the files related to the export-job.kjb job in Linux/Mac, type the following command:

   ```
   C:\temp\samples>Kitchen.bat /file:./export-job.kjb /
   export:sample-export
   ```

How it works...

There is no magic behind the creation of the archive containing our job and all of its referenced files of jobs and transformations. Everything is always made using the Apache VFS library to let PDI create the exported `.zip` archive file very easily. You can find more details about the Apache VFS library and how it works on the Apache website at `http://commons.apache.org/proper/commons-vfs`.

There's more...

Just a few words on some simple hints that can help you prevent unexpected behavior from the application.

Be careful when you are working with input steps that take an input as a set of files through a list. In our sample transformation, this is the case with the `TextInput` step. This step reads the file containing the customer dataset and sends the dataset into the transformation flow. All of these steps take as input a set of files to process. It could happen very easily that you forget an empty line at the very end of that file list as shown in the following screenshot:

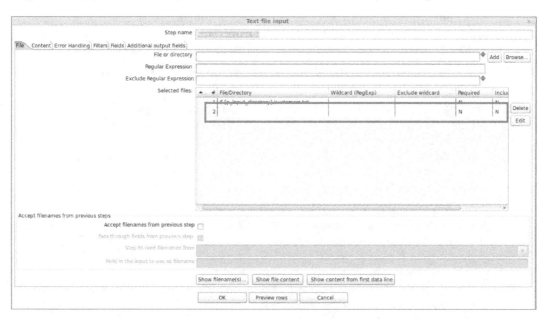

PDI does not give you an error while designing your transformation in Spoon if you leave the unused line highlighted in the preceding screenshot blank. But you could get into trouble if you try to export the job that uses that transformation by preventing the successful export of the job. So remember to check for this; and if these situations do exist, remember to clean it up.

Managing PDI processes return code (Simple)

This recipe covers an important aspect related to getting the return code that was obtained from the execution of our jobs. It gives you some advice on how to get it so that it could be used to determine if everything is going as expected. This recipe will work the same for both Kitchen and Pan; the only difference is in the name of the script's file used to start the process.

Getting ready

To get ready for this recipe, you need to check that the JAVA_HOME environment variable is set properly and then configure your environment variables so that the Kitchen script can start from anywhere without specifying the complete path to your PDI home directory. For details about these checks, refer to the recipe *Executing PDI jobs from a filesystem (Simple)*.

How to do it...

1. Every time you start a PDI process, either jobs or transformations, the script that started the job or the transformation gets back from PDI with a return code that gives an indication about whether the process terminated successfully or not.

2. In case the process terminated unsuccessfully, the code gives you an overall indication of what happened.

3. Looking on the Internet at the Pentaho wiki and at some blogs (an interesting article was published recently on this topic in *Diethard Steiner's* blog at `http://diethardsteiner.blogspot.it/2013/03/pentaho-kettle-pdi-get-pan-and-kitchen.html`), you can easily find a summary table that describes these error codes and their meaning, which we have described for reference purposes in the *There's more...* section.

4. To display this code on Linux/Mac, edit the `kitchen.sh` script and add the following command at the end of the PDI script. This command returns the exit code of the last called process:

   ```
   exit?1
   ```

5. To display this code on a Windows platform, edit the `Kitchen.bat` script and add the following command at the end of the PDI script. This command returns the exit code of the last called process:

   ```
   echo %ERRORLEVEL%
   ```

6. You can do the same with the Pan scripts. As soon as the script terminates, it displays the error code. You can try it out by adding it to your scripts and then calling one of your sample jobs or transformations. Getting this code is a very interesting thing because as soon as you call Kitchen or Pan scripts from inside another script, the caller is able to take action in case something goes wrong. This means that we can design an error handling strategy.

There's more...

It will be interesting to have a look at the summary of all the exit codes.

A summary of Kitchen/Pan exit codes

The following table summarizes all the exit codes with a brief explanation of their meanings:

Code	Description
0	The job/transformation ran without a problem.
1	An error occurred during processing.
2	An unexpected error occurred during loading/running of the job/transformation. Basically, it can be an error in the XML format, an error in reading the file, or it can denote that there are problems with the repository connection.
3	Unable to connect to a database, open a file, or other initialization errors.
7	The job/transformation couldn't be loaded from XML or the repository; basically, it could be that one of the plugins in the `plugins/` folder is not written correctly or is incompatible.
8	An error occurred while loading steps or plugins (an error in loading one of the plugins mostly).
9	Command line usage printing.

Scheduling PDI jobs and transformations (Intermediate)

ETL processes are always batch processes; you will launch them, and then at the very end you expect to get back the results. There is no kind of user interaction during the process's execution. Often, ETL processes can take quite some time to execute because they either work with a lot of data or they implement complex process rules that take a long time to execute. It is always a good idea to schedule them so that they can run whenever the system load is low. This last recipe guides you through how to schedule PDI jobs and transformations on Unix/Linux. As usual, anything is applicable for both jobs and transformations; the only difference is in the name of the script's file that is to be scheduled.

Getting ready

To get ready for this recipe, you need to check that the JAVA_HOME environment variable is set properly and then configure your environment variables so that the Kitchen script can start from anywhere without specifying the complete path to your PDI home directory. For details about these checks, refer to the recipe *Executing PDI jobs from a filesystem (Simple)*.

How to do it...

To schedule ETL processes on Linux, use the steps that follow:

1. To schedule ETL processes on Linux, we always use the cron scheduler. The task to do this is very easy, while understanding the syntax of the cron schedules is a bit more complicated.

2. To add a new schedule, you need to edit the crontab file; to do this, type the following command from the Linux command line:

   ```
   crontab -e
   ```

3. Depending on the distribution, you can also use some graphical tools to do the same, but as I always suggest, it is better to learn the command-line commands to give you complete freedom and portability.

4. To schedule a process, you need to specify the time at which the command will run. To do this, there is a particular syntax that lets you specify minutes, hours, the month date, and the month year. The format of any of these items is as follows:

   - **Minute**: The minute of the hour (0-59)
   - **Hour**: The hour of the day (0-23)
   - **Month day**: The day of the month (1-31)
   - **Month**: The month of the year (1-12)
   - **Weekday**: The day of the week (0-6, 0 = Sunday)

5. You can follow some simple rules to specify ranges or multiple values for any of the preceding items, summarized as follows:

   - Define ranges by giving the start and end values of the interval and separating them with a hyphen -
   - Define multiple values by separating the single values with a comma

6. So, let's suppose that we want to schedule a job in the `<book_samples>/sample1` directory called `export-job.kjb` to execute at every half an hour, at 20 and 50 minutes past the hour every day, except on weekends. To do this, you need to add a new schedule by typing the following command:

    ```
    20,50 * * * 1-5 <pdi_home>/kitchen.sh –file <books_samples>/
    export-job.kjb
    ```

7. After you have typed the command, save and quit the `crontab` editor by pressing the *Esc* key; then type `:wq`, and then press the *Enter* key. The schedule will immediately be available. As you can see, in this case, you need to specify the complete path to the PDI scripts and to the `export-job.kjb` job. Of course, scheduling a Pan script is just a matter of changing the script name.

8. Further references about how to schedule tasks with the `cron` scheduler can be found on Wikipedia at `http://en.wikipedia.org/wiki/Cron`.

To schedule ETL processes in Windows from **Task Scheduler**, use the steps that follow:

1. Go to **Control Panel | Administrative Tools | Task Scheduler**.

2. Select **Create a Basic Task** from the menu on the right.

3. The **Create Basic Task Wizard** dialog will be displayed. Enter the task name (for example, `Example PDI job`). Click on **Next**.

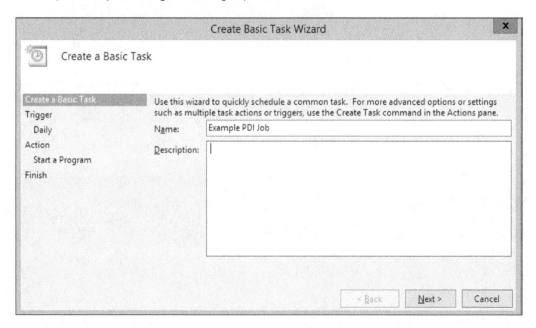

4. Select the schedule you want to apply. You can either select the schedule based on the calendar or on an event. Let us suppose our schedule is based on the calendar and we want our program to be scheduled daily. Select the **Daily** radio button and click on **Next**.

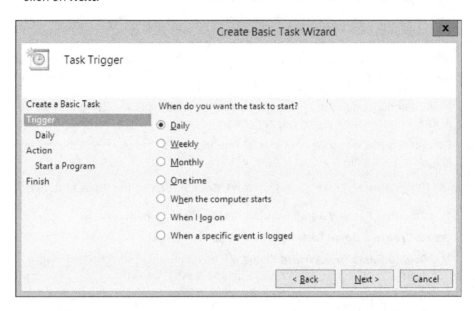

5. Insert the time you want the event to fire and its recurrence multiplicity (**Recur every**). We want, for example, the event to fire everyday at 4.00 A.M. Click on **Next**.

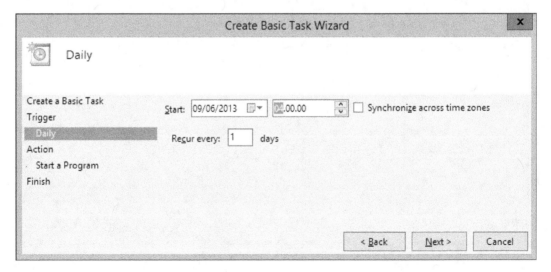

6. Select the action you want to accomplish; in our case, we select **Start a program**. Click on **Next**.

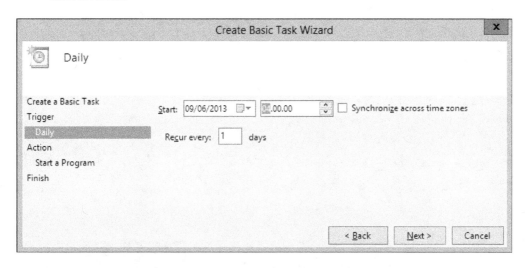

7. In the **Program/script** field, insert the full path and the name of the script you want to start (Kitchen.bat or Pan.bat). In the **Add arguments** field, insert the usual information you pass along to the Kitchen or Pan script to start your job or transformation properly. Click on **Next**.

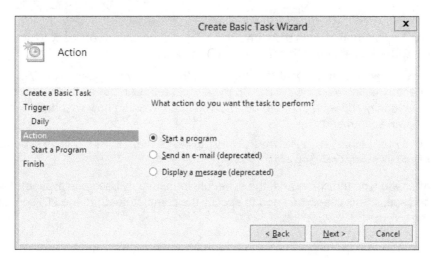

8. At the end, a summary dialog will open showing you all the parameters you inserted to completely define your schedule.

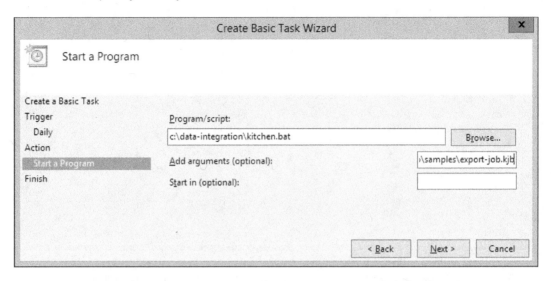

9. Click on **Finish**.

10. Your job will now appear in the list of waiting jobs.

To schedule ETL processes in Windows using the command line, use the following steps:

1. The `at` command works the same as `cron`, so it becomes very easy to schedule our job with Kitchen or our transformation with Pan.

2. Let's suppose that we want to schedule a job in the `<book_samples>/sample1` directory called `export-job.kjb` to be executed everyday at 8:00 AM with the exception of the weekends. To do this, you need to add a new schedule by typing the following command:

    ```
    at 8:00 /every:M,T,W,Th,F <pdi_home>\Kitchen.bat /file:<books_
    samples>\export-job.kjb
    ```

3. After you type the command, the schedule immediately becomes available. As you can see, in this case, you need to specify the complete path to the PDI scripts and to the `export-job.kjb` job.

There's more...

For Linux/Mac users, an interesting point is that whenever we execute a problem through a `cron` schedule, we get into trouble with our environment variables settings. Let's see how we can apply a little trick to solve all of this easily and without any pain.

Understanding crontab malfunctions

For Linux/Mac users, we can get into trouble because a `crontab` schedule for our application does not work properly. The reason for this is that `crontab` passes a minimal set of environment variables to our application. To look at this, you can add a dummy job and have the output of the environment variables written on a file as suggested by the following example:

```
* * * * * env > /tmp/env.log
```

To work around this, a first simple practice would be to remember to specify all of the environment variables used by your script in the script. If you are going to launch an application, wrap it in a little script where you will set all of your needed environment variables.

In case you don't want to redefine all of your environment variables, another option would be to add the following in the `crontab` scheduler before your command:

```
. $HOME/.profile.
```

An example of this is as follows:

```
0 5 * * * . $HOME/.profile; /path/to/command/to/run
```

This could be a simple way to access any environment variable defined for our user without having to respecify them in our script one by one.

Thank you for buying

Instant Pentaho Data Integration Kitchen

About Packt Publishing

Packt, pronounced 'packed', published its first book "*Mastering phpMyAdmin for Effective MySQL Management*" in April 2004 and subsequently continued to specialize in publishing highly focused books on specific technologies and solutions.

Our books and publications share the experiences of your fellow IT professionals in adapting and customizing today's systems, applications, and frameworks. Our solution based books give you the knowledge and power to customize the software and technologies you're using to get the job done. Packt books are more specific and less general than the IT books you have seen in the past. Our unique business model allows us to bring you more focused information, giving you more of what you need to know, and less of what you don't.

Packt is a modern, yet unique publishing company, which focuses on producing quality, cutting-edge books for communities of developers, administrators, and newbies alike. For more information, please visit our website: www.packtpub.com.

Writing for Packt

We welcome all inquiries from people who are interested in authoring. Book proposals should be sent to author@packtpub.com. If your book idea is still at an early stage and you would like to discuss it first before writing a formal book proposal, contact us; one of our commissioning editors will get in touch with you.

We're not just looking for published authors; if you have strong technical skills but no writing experience, our experienced editors can help you develop a writing career, or simply get some additional reward for your expertise.

Quick answers to common problems

**Pentaho Data
Integration 4 Cookbook**

Over 70 recipes to solve ETL problems using Pentaho Kettle

Adrián Sergio Pulvirenti
María Carina Roldán

Pentaho Data Integration 4 Cookbook

ISBN: 978-1-84951-524-5   Paperback: 352 pages

Over 70 recipes to solve ETL problems using
Pentaho Kettle

1. Manipulate your data by exploring, transforming, validating, integrating, and more

2. Work with all kinds of data sources such as databases, plain files, and XML structures among others

3. Use Kettle in integration with other components of the Pentaho Business Intelligence Suite

4. Each recipe is a carefully organized sequence of instructions packed with screenshots, tables, and tips to complete the task as efficiently as possible

Learn by doing: less theory, more results

**Pentaho 4.0 Reporting
by Example**

Create high-quality, professional standard reports using today's most-popular open source reporting tool

Beginner's Guide

Mariano García Mattío
Ing. Bernabeu R. Darío

Pentaho 4.0 Reporting by Example: Beginner's Guide

ISBN: 978-1-78216-224-7   Paperback: 316 pages

Create high-quality, professional standard reports using today's most-popular open source reporting tool

1. Install and configure PRD in Linux and Windows

2. Create complex reports using relational data sources

3. Produce reports with groups, aggregate functions, parameters, graphics, and sparklines

4. Install and configure Pentaho BI Server to execute PRD reports

Please check **www.PacktPub.com** for information on our titles

OSWorkflow

ISBN: 978-1-84719-152-6   Paperback: 212 pages

A guide for Java developers and architects to integrating open-source Business Process Management

1. Basics of OSWorkflow

2. Integrating business rules with Drools

3. Task scheduling with Quartz

Pentaho Reporting 3.5 for Java Developers

ISBN: 978-1-84719-319-3   Paperback: 384 pages

Create advanced reports, including cross tabs, sub-reports, and charts that connect to practically any data source using open source Pentaho Reporting

1. Create great-looking enterprise reports in PDF, Excel, and HTML with Pentaho's Open Source Reporting Suite, and integrate report generation into your existing Java application with minimal hassle

2. Use data source options to develop advanced graphs, graphics, cross tabs, and sub-reports

3. Dive deeply into the Pentaho Reporting Engine's XML and Java APIs to create dynamic reports

Please check **www.PacktPub.com** for information on our titles

www.ingramcontent.com/pod-product-compliance
Lightning Source LLC
LaVergne TN
LVHW080104070326
832902LV00014B/2420